In The Wild

Lions

Claire Robinson

Heinemann Library
Chicago, Illinois

© 1997 Reed Educational & Professional Publishing
Published by Heinemann Library,
an imprint of Reed Educational & Professional Publishing,
Chicago, IL
Customer Service: 888-454-2279
Visit our website at www.heinemannlibrary.com

Printed and bound in China by South China Printing Company.
Designed by Celia Floyd
Cover design by Lucy Smith

06 05

10 9 8 7

The Library of Congress has cataloged the hardcover version of this book as follows:
Library of Congress Cataloging-in-Publication Data

Robinson, Claire, 1955-
    Lions / Claire Robinson.
        p.   cm. -- (In the wild)
    Includes bibliographical references (p.   ) and index.
    Summary: Describes, in simple text and illustrations, the physical
charactistics, natural environment, and habits of a pride of wild
lions.
    ISBN 1-57572-132-5 (lib. bdg.)
    1. Lions--Juvenile literature.   [1. Lions.]   I. Title.
II. Series: Robinson, Claire, 1955-   In the wild.
QL737.C23R623   1997
599. 757--dc21   97-12310
                                                          CIP
                                                          AC
Paperback ISBN 1-57572-467-7

Acknowledgments
The author and publishers are grateful to the following for permission to reproduce copyright
photographs:
Bruce Coleman Ltd./Christer Fredriksson, p. 12; Rod Williams, p. 5 right; FLPA/David Hosking
p. 7; Terry Whitaker, p. 4; NHPA/Anthony Bannister, p. 5; Oxford Scientific Films/Jen and Des
Bartlett, p. 21; David Cayless, pp. 8, 17; David Cura, p. 10; Mark Deeble and Victoria Stone, p.
23; Gregory D. Dimijian, p. 16; John Downer, p. 9; David Hamman, p. 19; Mike Hill, p. 18; Lee
Lyon/Survival, p. 15; Sian Osolinski, p. 22; Richard Packwood, p. 13; Norbert Rosing, pp. 14,
20; Edwin Sadd, p. 11; Kjell Sanored, p. 4; Claire Robinson, p. 6.

Cover photo: Oxford Scientific Films

Special thanks to Oxford Scientific Films

Every effort has been made to contact copyright holders of any material reproduced in this
book. Any omissions will be rectified in subsequent printings if notice is given to the publisher.

Some words are shown in bold, **like this**. You can find out
what they mean by looking in the glossary.

Contents

Relatives

Lions are a type of big cat. There are seven kinds of big cats and 29 kinds of small cats. You can see some cats here.

lion

tiger

caracal

desert cat

Caracals and desert cats are types of small cats.

Lions are the only cats that live in large families, or **prides**. What's it like to live in a pride of lions?

5

Where Lions Live

These lions live on the sunny **grasslands** of Africa. Zebras, giraffes, elephants, and antelope live here too.

Each lion **pride** lives on its own stretch of grassland. This area of land is called a **territory**.

The Pride

The largest adult males protect the **pride**. Their hairy manes make them look strong and fierce.

There are lots of females in the pride.
They care for the **cubs** and do most
of the hunting.

Sleeping

Like all cats, the lions spend most of their day resting. They love the warmth of the sun.

This **cub** is fast asleep in a tree. Look at the spotted pattern in his coat. It keeps him hidden from **predators**.

Hunting

The **pride** is hungry. The lioness **stalks** a **herd** of buffalo, keeping her head and body low in the grass.

Her sisters are ready to join her in the hunt. They work well as a team.

Eating

The **herd** panics. The lioness leaps to bring down a buffalo with her strong paws and sharp claws.

The big lions push forward to eat.
Sometimes there is not much meat left for
the **cubs**.

Rest and Roar

The lions have eaten well today. They are resting. They don't need to hunt for another three or four days.

The lions see some strange male lions on their **territory**. They roar to scare them away.

Babies

One of the lionesses has given birth to **cubs**. She keeps them close by her side.

The cubs are always hungry. Their
mother lies back and feeds them with
her milk.

Growing Up

The lioness keeps a close eye on her **cubs**. To move them to a safer place, she carries them gently in her mouth.

As the cubs grow up, they learn to be adult lions. They love to play fighting and hunting games.

Lion Facts

- Lions have four sharp **canine teeth** for killing their **prey**.

- Lions live for about 15 years.

- Lionesses give birth to a litter of **cubs**. Usually there are two or three cubs in a **litter**.

- The females in a **pride** are all related. Sometimes they feed each others' cubs.

- The females own the **territory**. The adult males live there until stronger males take their place in the pride.

- Most lions live in Africa, but there is a rare Asian lion that is only found in the Gir Forest in India.

Glossary

canine teeth   Long, pointed teeth.
cub   Baby lion.
grassland   Very large area of grass.
herd   Large group of animals that live together, such as zebras and antelope.
litter   Lion cubs born at the same time.
predators   Animals that hunt other animals for food.
prey   Animal hunted as food.
pride   Family, or group of lions.
stalk   To follow something quietly, keeping out of sight.
territory   Area of land that animals see as their own.

Index

More Books To Read

Hoffman, Mary. *Lion*. Austin, Tex.: Raintree Steck-Vaughn, 1985.
Stone, Lynn. *Lions*. Vero Beach, Fla.: Rourke, 1989.
Urquhart, Jennifer C. *Lions and Tigers and Leopards*. Washington, D. C. : National Geographic Society, 1990.